Kismet

page publishing

Kismet

DIPA SARKAR-DEY

PAGE PUBLISHING
Conneaut Lake, PA

First originally published by Page Publishing 2022

ISBN 979-8-88654-489-3 (pbk)
ISBN 979-8-88654-490-9 (digital)
Library of Congress Control Number: 2022921335

Contents

Acknowledgments

I am incredibly indebted to my mentor, Prof. Karen Fish, who introduced me to the world of poetry. Her valuable advice and comments made the book possible. I am obliged to Prof. Teresa Ryan, who inspired me to write poetry.

I am lucky that my husband, Gautam, not only encouraged me to write but also read them diligently. His skillful reading helped me to correct the mistakes. I am lovingly thankful to my daughter, Prajna—who, in her busy schedule, always finds time to review my writing—and my son, Atish, for his valuable suggestions.

I am grateful for all of the support and advice I received from the editors and artists of Page Publishing.

Finally, I am thankful to my family members Rahul, Roli, Edie, Leela, and Ishani, and my siblings and their families who always supported me with new adventures.

CHAPTER 1

War and Peace

A bird was sitting on the tulip tree
Its partner was waiting on the wisteria vine.
A squirrel was playing on the tulip tree
Noticed the bird and was delighted.
Suddenly an ambulance appeared
Blasting its siren, shaking the neighborhood.
The man of the house had a heart attack
The paramedics gave mouth-to-mouth resuscitation
That started his heart racing like a train.
The bird flew away
The unlucky squirrel jumped in vain.

Fearsome Night

My face was serene with a Mona Lisa smile; inside though, all the blood vessels were throbbing like boiling tomato sauce. I was in the Pak Army barracks with my father and sister. Two captains invited us for dinner. They were not wearing their uniforms. I was eighteen, my sister sixteen. There were whisky bottles, glasses, a bowl of peanuts, and a pistol on the table. They were drinking and offered us drinks. We politely ignored the offer. The room was dimly lit. Pictures of the president and the founding father were on the wall. Mosquito-repelling coils were burning at the corners. Fragrance of honeysuckle and tuberose numbed our nerves. The butler brought beef curry, fried okra, and naan for dinner. We didn't have any appetite but picked naan and okra to oblige. Beef was prohibited by religion.

There was small talk and then their winning spree against Mukti Bahini. We were listening and punctuated our listening with an occasional yes or no. A couple of weeks prior, my father witnessed their tortures. He watched as others were poked with bayonets and beat with bamboo canes. I saw my father's eyes burn like coals and noticed his lips tremble. I guessed he was praying for our lives. Suddenly one of the captains got up and called the driver. I felt it in my body, the calm like the calmness after a hurricane. A ray of moonlight started dancing on the floor.

Moment of Grace

I was lying on the bed moaning with my son at my side.
I broke my leg playing *kabaddi* with my friends
A few days prior at a picnic.
I felt guilty for his helping hand
While his sister was having fun at a summer camp.
I asked, "Would you like to visit your friend's house?"
Holding my leg, he didn't answer.
It was a muggy July afternoon.

"Son, would you like to visit your friend's house?"
He walked away in silence.
I heard him doing something in the kitchen
When he returned, he had two sandwiches.
"Son, I am asking you a simple question
But you are doing everything without giving me an answer."

He divulged, "I don't know how should I respond to your question
I really want to go to my friend's house
But who would take care of you while I am out?"
Tears streamed down my face
Since he was only a little boy, a little boy of eight.
His compassion filled my heart and I
Thanked God for His wonderful creation.

Dream

I was struck with a blow, a big hole in my heart
Over the loss of my mentor, friend, guidance counselor.
He sowed the seed of equality of genders
Work hard and achieve whatever you want.
Ma called and consoled me with her soft voice
When she herself needed comfort the most.
She was the one who had lost her companion
A passionate one took care of her for more than fifty years.
My mother and I were ten thousand miles apart
Sobbing quietly without seeing each other,
Both at a loss of this losing.

I saw my father walking with his father
Along the bank of a river covered with water lilies
My father and his father had calm, serene faces.
I was delighted to see them completely in peace
They had gone through so many ups and downs
It was hard to comprehend their mental strength.

They smiled noticing me watching
Started walking toward me in long strides
"Don't worry, little girl, we would be with you all the time."
Suddenly, it was as if someone had pushed me
And I was falling like a feather through the clouds
When I touched the ground, I woke up with a jolt.

That Season

The Pak Army had set fire at lumberyards and in the nearby slums of Nayapara, at the outskirt of Dhaka City. We all gathered on the balcony and heard screaming. A few hours ago, my brother came home. He was a medical college student. In anatomy classes, he used to cut dead bodies. Yet on that day, he threw up after he encountered mutilated bodies on the street. The sun was just on the horizon. The soft orange color of the going-down sun and the bright orange from the fire enchanted the evening sky. It was spring. The flamboyant bloomed. The red color of the flowers and the fragrance from the exotic flowers made the air heavenly. However, the southwest breeze of spring felt like carrying the fire toward our house. We were all scared, and an eerie silence in the house made all of us frozen. Suddenly my younger sister started crying. She was a teenager and had trouble with the ferocity of the scenery. Then, my father, with his harsh voice, started singing a devotional song.

Stupidity

The teacher had just left the classroom.
I was sitting in a circle with Dana, Era, and Moyna.
We made fun of each other,
Giggling and rolling over.

Next period's teacher was out on a vacation
Instead of a substitute, the class captain was in charge.
She tried hard to control the students
That made the entire class more gregarious.

Four of us didn't pay attention to the others
Looked through the window, made fun of the passersby.
"Let's have a cigar," Dana suggested
We jumped up. We were in fifth grade.
In a chorus we shouted, "Oh, sure,"
Not thinking of being found out or the punishments afterward.

Dana lit the cigar and handed it to me
I puffed and then coughed and hacked like my old granddaddy.
Dana snatched the cigar with frustration
And inhaled like a Marlboro Man.
But she did not know how to exhale
And scared us with her red choked face.

The next-door teacher, an ill-tempered lady
Carried a cane and used it to discipline.
She was disturbed by the unruly noise
Huffing and puffing with an uproar
And slashing the air with her cane
Appeared at our classroom door.
We all stood up to greet her
She smelled cigar and was positively dumbstruck.

Four of us were suspended for a week
A letter from the school carried the news.
The letter mentioned my unthinkable behavior
As I was quieter and smarter than the others.

My father was confused by the letter
No one in my family had ever smoked a cigar.
The punishment I received
Beyond your imagination, without any mercy.

Land of Equality

Higher studies brought me to the USA
Leaving everyone eight thousand miles away.
It was in the eighties—without YouTube, Facebook, or WhatsApp.
The communication was all via snail mail.
It took about a month to know well-being.
Occasional phone calls to hear the voices
I could not afford frequent calls on the academic stipends.

The fast-paced lifestyle of the new country
Made me homesick every night.
However, each new morning brought new hope
And I found delight in chores.
Amazed by my own cooking and cleaning.
Back home I had only one chore to do—study.
The rest was all done by someone else
I had never paid attention.

Met Rajiv, a handsome man at a college social
Came a couple of years earlier
From my country but from a different state.
Our mother languages and religions were different
But it didn't stop us from becoming good friends.

Out of the blue, he proposed to me and
I accepted without consulting my parents.
Both sides were furious
Nonetheless, we became husband and wife.
Our parents soon embraced our union
And arranged a beautiful wedding reception afterward.

Marrying Rajiv was the best thing that happened in my life.
In the land of equality—no eyebrows raised, no questions asked
Everyone was happy to embrace our union.

Visitation

Felt energetic after a long sickness
Got up and looked in the mirror
Bewildered by seeing my *thamma*, my *thamma*
In the mirror smiling at me.
She looked exactly the way
When I met her last time.

A relief map resembled her face
With all the wrinkles and bumps.
The eyes were deep pit
Thank God she wore glasses.
The fibers of the rug
I was standing on
Resembled the coarse grayish-blond hair.
The veins on her hand
Bulged out through the thin pale skin.
The sagging neck was full of speckles
And a little hunchback.

I actually asked, "*Thamma*, what are you doing here?"
After my nerves had come down.
"Darling, with whom are you talking?"
Shaken by the question
Saw the husband behind *thamma*.

Oh, God! I saw my own reflection
Never ever realized I had aged.
Reminiscing the days I visited her

When I was ten and thought
I knew my body—knew my body would surely
Never, never be thamma's.[1]

---

[1] The line in italics is from the poem "Visiting" by Dr. Karen Fish *Thamma—*
father's mother

Freedom

———

14

I always wanted to live like a free bird
Gliding through the air.
But the life I lived shackled my feet.

My mother taught me to be nice
Even when someone is insulted or bullied, with a big smile.
I diligently followed Ma's advice
Pretended to be happy all the time.

One day it shattered like a broken window
Left me alone all of a sudden.
I was walking along a slippery road
Like a toddler without any balance.

Out of the blue I was grabbed by two strong hands
Whispered, "Lean on me to get the balance."
It felt like clearing, freshening even a rainbow after the rain
Then, I became the free bird I had always craved.

Bodacious Day

Denied, one word, one ferocious word
INS officer stamped the word
On our application for a permanent residency visa.
The reason: incomplete application,
No longer accepting affidavit of birth
In lieu of a legal birth certificate.
With a broken heart we came back home.

After lunch I went out to check the mailbox,
Hollered, "Eureka, eureka," like Archimedes
When I found peeking through the junk mail
A letter from the DC embassy of my native country.
The letter reinforced that affidavit of birth
Was considered a legal birth certificate
During the period of our births.

Without wasting any time, we went back the very same day to the INS office
And resubmitted the application with the embassy letter.
Half an hour later, we were instructed to go upstairs
A gentleman wearing uniform interrogated us.
He asked plain but intimate questions,
"Where and how did you meet your husband?
What is your son's favorite TV show?"
He grilled us separately for about an hour
Then stamped on our passport
Two words, two legal words
Changed our lives like a fairy tale.
Work permitted.

First Meeting

My eyes were looking for you at the airport to meet you in person after many hours of conversation. None of us had a smartphone then but a flip cell phone. We talked hours after hours, three or four times a day. One day you called me on your way to visit a friend. Almost four hours of drive felt like a blink of an eye. I do not recall the content of our conversation, yet it continued a few more hours after your arrival. I went to a conference, and you offered me to pick you up from the airport on my return.

The day before, I spent a fortune at the hotel parlor, to enhance my outer appearances. I wanted to inflate your desire of longing for me like a deprived soul meeting the first time the soul mate. You were strolling a few feet away from the luggage conveyer belt and approached me slowly with lots of hesitation. We didn't see each other's photograph; we were relying on our self-description. I shook your hands confirming my identity. Your look assured me of the success of my investment. We were talking and laughing with holding each other's hands waiting for the shuttle to take us to the parking lot. On the shuttle, you suddenly pecked on my cheek. I blushed like a teenager having the first kiss.

Grief

At your funeral when everyone was praising you
I was cussing you for the cruelty of leaving me.
I have been in a wheelchair for the last thirty years
Yet you loved me, took care of me without regret.

You looked stunning in the army uniform
When I first met you at my friend's house.
You came home after serving two years in Vietnam
I was listening to your stories sitting in a corner.
Suddenly our eyes met, and I saw my reflection
In your deep blue eyes, I was a girl with an innocent smile.

Next time I ran into you at a poetry class in college
The professor was reciting "Ode to a Nightingale" by Keats.
His voice echoing in the classroom
But I was looking at you with numbness pains.
You couldn't ignore my beauty and attraction
Easily butchered yourself under my magic spell of love.

We got married and had three children
Together we made our life, made in heaven.
One terrible night I started vomiting and had a fever
An excruciating headache and stiffness in the legs.
The doctor diagnosed it to be polio
My parents were not keen on vaccinating children.

You took care of me
Still couldn't erase the destiny of my losing my legs.
You were only thirty-eight at that time
Began taking care of a *disabled wife*.
I learned to take care of myself sitting on the chair
Even continued my teaching without disruption.

For forty years you stood by my side
Never ever thought of leaving me, leaving me in disgrace.
I know it was my destiny to live without you
Nonetheless I feel like screaming, "Why? Why me?"

Celebration

An old man was riding a rickshaw
Covering his head and neck with a scarf.
It was December, he was shivering
But couldn't stay home—
Wanted to devour the moment of triumph.
His cheeks were guttered with tears,
I photographed him
To capture the significant moment.

The armies discarded their uniforms
Tried to erase their identities.
I quickly took a snapshot of their deception.
The photograph became the symbol
Of cowardness of a skilled army battalion
Who surrendered to a bunch of idiots—
Picked up rifles, manufactured homemade bombs.

I walked mile after mile without any discomfort
Got the strength from the cheering crowd.
At dusk when the birds were returning home
A few teenagers lighted twigs, rags, and papers
In the middle of a field near a river.
They were singing and dancing around the blaze without any fear.
No one realized, no one anticipated that just yesterday
They were all on the list of a killing spree.

Miracle

The daily evening news on the Ukraine war
Reminding me of the time of war
Fifty years ago, ten thousand miles away.
The gruesome pictures guttered me with tears.
Volunteers were cleaning up the debris
After the heavy bombing and delighted,
When found a child in a huddle of rags.
A journalist took a snapshot of the child
To show the world a miracle of life.
One day on a happy note, the news
Showed a little boy riding a chariot
Sitting on his father's lap and
His mother knitting a winter cap.

Wailea Beach

Holding your hand tightly
We walked along the Wailea beach
Through ankle-deep water with bare feet.
The waves washing away and replenishing
The smooth sands gently messaged our bare feet.
Suddenly the waves became stronger
Roaring like a mad elephant
Caused us to move away from the tide line.

The tourist with expensive cameras
Gathered along the roadside
To capture the end of the day.
The horizon divided the bright yellowish red ball
And we were mesmerized by half of the ball in the sky
And the other half underwater.

The full moon in the opposite sky
Peeping through a coconut tree full of coconuts.
Purple and white bougainvillea
Added extra beauty.

I almost crushed your hand with excitement
You neither disturbed me nor said a word
Continued walking by my side along the beach
Gently unhinged my strong grab.

Better World

The bride was wearing a scarlet *banarasi* saree, and an artist decorated her face with sandalwood paste. She was sitting like a cuddly poodle. Her friends teasing her, and she was enjoying their erotic comments. Her sister came in and whispered to her. Suddenly, she turned into a ferocious tigress. She ran into the room decorated with flowers where the groom was sitting like a king on a throne. The bride's father was adjuring to the groom to stop his uncle who threatened to leave, if the remaining dowry was not paid before the wedding.

"Please son, I beg of you don't make my daughter *lagnabhrasta*.[2] No one will marry her again. I promise to give you the remaining dowry in a few months." Without any warning, the fuming bride slapped the groom and sternly told him to leave promptly with all his friends and relatives. With this, her father started screaming and crying like a lunatic, "What have you done? How could I face society?" The incident became a colorful party-energizing story. In a few years, another proposal came. Would-be groom eager to marry the girl. He was fascinated by the girl's courage. Angels in heaven bellowed the conchs.

---

[2] *lagnabhrasta*—a bride who missed the wedding time

Kismet

Shayma and Radha, two sisters, two years apart
Were named after two goddesses their parents worshiped.
Unfortunately those names reflected skin color,
Shayma, the older one dark-skinned
Radha with lighter skin tone.

There was no animosity between the sisters
Parents loved them equally without reservation.
Growing up, Shayma occasionally heard a comment
"It would be difficult to find a nice groom for her,"
From a visiting family member or a neighbor.
She never paid any attention to those comments
Since she also heard praises of her sharp features
And dazzling eyes like a doe.

The girls inherited musical talents from parents
Mother was a vocalist and father a flutist.
Radha had a melodious voice and
Shayma played *tabla* to add rhythm.
Most of the evenings four of them
Had a mini concert at their home
Travelers were halted by the harmonious tune.

Shayma received more attention from Father
Because of her curious and scientific mind
Radha was Mother's favorite
For her artistic talents and compassion.
Shayma studied engineering like her father
Radha studied to be a social worker.
Both of the girls were talented
Received handsome government scholarship
Parents didn't pay a dime for education.

Shayma began working after completing her degree
Radha was still continuing her education.
An aunt brought a marriage proposal for Shayma
Would-be groom, Amol, was a budding professor.
A day was fixed for Amol and his family
To visit Shayma's house to meet her and the family.

On the day of the visit, the house was cleaned spic-and-span
The maids were scolded for not paying attention to tiny details.
Mother prepared exotic dishes
Father went out to buy expensive sweets for the guests.
Shayma wore a silk saree, a light makeup with eyeliner
And put a *bindi* on the forehead matching the saree color.
Looking at her, Mother thought,
No one could deny this exquisite woman.

The guests arrived two hours later
No one was annoyed by their behavior
Everyone was there to please them.
Shayma's parents were impressed by the visitors
Found them courteous and easygoing people.
Maid brought tea and the delicious dishes
Shayma arrived with Radha with a tray of sweets.
Amol was small-talking with the sisters
With his eyes gazing at Radha.
The meeting ended with a musical presentation
The guests left with a marking impression.

Shayma was happy to meet Amol
She found him handsome, charming, and thoughtful
At night in sleep she dreamt of a life with him.

The next day a call came from Amol's mother
To fix a wedding date with Radha immediately,
Amol was leaving the country for higher studies.
Shayma's mother was confused by the request

Soon found out it was Amol's choice.
Shayma was heartbroken by the news
But able to hide her disappointment
Agreed to arrange the wedding with Radha.

On the wedding day Shayma was gregarious
Charmed everyone with her witty conversations.
She danced with old and young
Parents were happy to see her jovial
Couldn't recognize her bleeding heart.

After the wedding, lots of proposals came
Many of them were better than Amol
Shayma refused all of them.
She was determined not to be humiliated
By another man.
A colleague at work became friendly with her
Impressed her with his good looks and humor.
She started dating him behind her parents' back
Within a year became husband and wife.
It was a civil marriage in front of a judge
Fortunately parents were there as witnesses.

Radha and Amol settled in the new country
Couldn't find time to visit home.
Ten years passed by, they became parents
In school, children were learning their ancestry.
That prompted them to plan for a trip
To show the children their ancestral home.

Shayma with her husband went to the airport
To receive Radha and her family.
Radha came out with a big smile
Hugged and kissed Shayma like the old days.
Radha looked exactly the same when she left
Shayma was pleased to see Radha's children.

However, her eyes were searching for Amol
Couldn't locate him among the crowd.
Suddenly the children ran to their father
Who came out pushing the luggage cart.
Shayma was shocked to see
A bald-headed man with a beer belly.
She looked at her husband standing nearby
Impressed by his hairy head and athletic physique.
She forgot all the humiliation and
Thanked God for Amol's rejection.

CHAPTER 2

Nirvana

I like to be reborn again and again
Without achieving *Nirvana* or *Moksha.*
Life is full of joy and suffering
Want to experience them equally
As many lifetimes as possible.

The red lava erupted from a volcano
Gave an uncanny beauty to the nature
No artist could ever portray such scenery.
It ruined everything on its way
But formed most fertile soils on earth
Cultivating the land produced food and civilization.

A pandemic devastated the world
Killed and disabled millions of young and old.
A new mRNA vaccine brought hope
Paved a way for the recovery in future.

Imagining a life living alone
When only had experiences living with many
Shook the world underneath like an earthquake.
Yet when it had happened
Oh, what a relief it was! Beyond imagination.

I want to live catastrophic situations again and again
Praying to the Ishwar for removing the obstacles
Thankful to the Ishwar for the pleasing experiences
Without a life, there is no Ishwar.

Nataraja

He stands on a lotus pedestal, lifting the left leg
The right leg is balancing on a dwarf, symbolizing ignorance.
Nataraja is the cosmic dancer
His dance preserves the existence of the universe,
Ultimately one day the dance will destroy the universe.

We see Lord Shiva, one of the Trinities of Hinduism,
Dancing in one of the poses of the *Natya Shastra*.
The dance commands the souls to go above the materialistic desire
The circular frame of flame surrounding his rhythmic play
Represents the source of all movements in the universe.
In his four hands is the depiction of creation, destruction, rhythm,
and blessings.
The tourists are dumbfounded to see this statue
Within the grounds of CERN, instead of a temple or a museum
But the statue is a metaphor for the study of the cosmic dance of
subatomic particles.
The sculpture with its style and proportions
Intertwined the art of dance and religion.

In distress we find strength analyzing Nataraja here—
After destruction a new creation certainly will appear.

My Love

My love for you felt like a tsunami
coming in huge unstoppable waves.
Tornado love destroying funneling air.

Progressively my love for you—an earthquake
with its vigorous shake.

Later, the love was a snowstorm glowing
and whiting all else out.
But sometimes, my love is like a thunder
a monstrous call.

Increasingly, my love for you, a lightning
inciting jagged, bright twinkling.
Or…love for you might be a cherry blossom
poised, an elegant flower.

With you it's cozy living sitting on the sofa
with conversation of laughter and grief.
This lifelong love for you is really like a prayer
spooling forward, murmuring, soothing
your voice, my comfort.

Morning

The sunny side is up and flaring
Soft orange light as the clear blue sky goes to dreamland.
Reflection on the water lures the fish, frogs to the surface.
The water has a ripple effect—actual breath.
Water lilies open to show their insides—that gorgeous pink
Water hyacinths brag purple flowers.
Ducks cruise in small groups.
A young man rows a boat with a white sail
Singing a folk song, his voice exalted.

Highlighting each and every droplet, a tiny rainbow.
Butterflies wing from flower to bud under
The incessant bird song.
There is even an occasional woodpecker to hammer a tree.
Despite the beauty—joggers and walkers continue
With their daily rituals of practice, occasionally
Pausing to sit on the bank. It all reminds me of the lyrics from the
movie Oklahoma,
"Oh, what a beautiful morning."

Autumn

Everyone is ready to welcome Goddess Durga
Who will kill all the demons in life
And bring peace and prosperity to humankind.

Bright blue sky with occasional clouds
The golden harvest on the green fields
And soft breeze
Like a mother's touch on a sick child
The arrival of autumn in Bengal.

Couples longing for intimate touches
Sit on the park benches
After the hot and humid summer days.

In the faraway corner under a tree
A white velvet carpet with orange patches
Formed by the fallen *Shiuli* flowers,
Bloomed last evening.
The fragrance of the flowers
Make the young and old romantic.

A young girl trying to sell garlands
"Ten rupees only buy it for her."

Life

—

A fall morning
We were all home-bound for the pandemic.
Sitting on a sofa on our backyard deck
Daydreaming our days with family and friends.
Suddenly a wind came with a musical hymn
Causing the leaves to rain down like rain.
The leaves flew like feathers, down, down all over my head
The bunnies started jumping and running following them.

Enjoying the beauty of the nature with all my senses
And saw a hummingbird sucking nectars from a flowering plant.
It was not bothered by the falling leaves
But doing its job, flapping those wings so fast it's all blur.
The wind stopped and became a breeze
And I started to count all the falling leaves one, two, three.

Wondering whether the remaining leaves on the tree
Were sad and mourning for their fallen nearest and dearest ones.
Then, I looked up, and saw a leaf, waving at me—showing its strength
At that moment, the wind became strong, detached the leaf from the tree.
While falling, the leaf whispered, that I should not feel sorry for
Thousands of new leaves would appear in the next spring.

Spring Flowers

Daffodils, *fluttering and dancing in the breeze*[3]
On the front yard reminding us of spring.
The gray depressing days of winter erased
The yellow flowers on green stems
Made a miracle.
In a few weeks all the cherry trees
The neighborhood bloomed
No need to visit DC for cherry blossom.
Purple, orange, pink, red, and white tulips
Substituted the missing yellow and overtook the landscape.
Then, azaleas added more colors,
Strollers could not resist noticing.
Princess tree-shaded purple flowers
On the chartreuse spring grass;
Red honeysuckle, purple wisteria, and lavender lilac
Made the backyard.
Friends praised my green thumb
As we sat idly drinking tea on the deck
It felt all my hard work was overpaid.

---

[3]   Italicized line is from "Daffodils" by William Wordsworth

Snow Day

Saw the notification when the alarm rang
Classes canceled.
Tossing and turning for a while then got up.
The unexpected holiday like winning a small lotto.

Two feet of snow fell yesterday
The piles of snow on the driveway
Cautioned me not to get out.
Ramon was still in bed
Made a cup of coffee, looked through the window.
Numerous tiny rainbows were dazzling
Formed by the sunlight reflecting on the snow.

Suddenly I saw a tiny bird on the banister
Flapping the wings and looking around.
The small bird reminded me of when I was alone
Eating dinner, no one asking, "How was your day?"

"Would you like to have another cup?"
Ramon's inquiry brought me back to the real world.
The bare trees covered with snow,
Looked like a Picasso.

Summer Break

On the train traveling for the first time myself
Escorted by a family friend,
Put my head on the windowsill
For the soft summer breeze.
I was visiting my grandparents' home
During summer vacation.

Clank, clank, clank, the train made noise
Going on the bridge over the Brahmaputra River.
On the bank a little girl sat quietly
A fisherman was pulling the net with a big catch.
The faraway land looked like a yellow carpet
Noticed yellow mustard flowers closer.
A wedding procession with a band party
Stopped at the railway crossing,
The bride moved her red veil to see the train.

Vendors selling food, jewelry, toys, and herbal medicines
Got up when we stopped at stations along the route.
It was all boisterous jingles sung to attract purchases
Ignored Ma's advice and bought a doll, a flute, and a bracelet.

I saw my grandpa's smiling face at the station first then,
Rode a rickshaw along the bank of a canal.
Children were jumping and swimming in the water
A fabulous musty aroma in the air,
From the decaying leaves of the plants in water.

Granny welcomed me with a *barfi* in my mouth
She made it with milk, coconut, and sugar.
With a mouth full described my train journey recounted

The scene of a naked little boy jumped into water
A lady madly screamed raising both the hands
And was stopped for the fear of choking.

As the dusk approached Granny lit a *diya* on the *tulsi bedi*
She and Grandpa sang devotional songs for the deities.
Their voices and musical instruments like nothing I'd known,
Familiar and utterly different—at the same time.
I was surprised by the talent for the first time in my life.

With my grandparents, above all,
I received undivided love and attention.
With me still is the scent of the oil in the *diya,*
How their faces were lighted up with successes
And then swallowed by darkness with losses.
Their voices indicating how close they were
Throughout their lives for forty years.

Enjoyed the quiet serene rural life
Pitter-patter of the raindrops, murmur of the trees.
The winking of the fireflies in a moonless night
Couldn't be found in the bustling lighted city life.

Appointment

Ophthalmologist's office: a diagramed human eye on the wall
Projected fifty times its normal size.
"My eyes look exactly the same as before,
No pain, no redness, no itching, no scratchy feeling
Why do I have foggy vision?
Why do I have hard time seeing and driving at night?"
The front part of the eye as seen in a mirror
Includes the iris, cornea, pupil, sclera, and conjunctiva
Pointing to the diagram, ophthalmologist explained
Were not the causes of my vision problems.

Oedipus, the hero in Greek legend unknowingly
Killed his father and married his mother.
When he realized his dirty work
He put his eyes out to punish himself.

My friend Rana lost one eye in a road accident
An ocular prosthesis implanted in the eye socket.
He couldn't see with it but an unknown person
Couldn't find any difference.

My father's eyes felt like burning me into ashes
When he learned about my mischievous deeds.
The same eyes showed affection and praises
When he learned about my achievements.

I was wondering about the eye stories
When the ophthalmologist's voice brought back our conversation.
"Your vision problem lied on the back,
Behind the iris and pupil lies the lens
Which became cloudy, the cause of the problem."
A surgery would require removing the lens

They'd replace it with an intraocular lens.
It would be a minor surgery not to worry
Ophthalmologist's diagnosis made me euphoric.

My husband was delighted to see my smiling face
I had an edgy face before going to the ophthalmologists.

Snail

His hands were muscular
With long thin fingers like an artist.
He was kneading clay to make potteries.
His creation reminded me of a giant snail
In the jungles of Masai Mara.
"It looks like a giant African snail?"
He looked up with a wicked smile
"It is a vase; buy three get one free."

Mail

Among the mails a red card with my name on it
Waving at me to open, I ignored the rest.
It came from my son and his lovely wife
It felt heavier than the usual greeting cards.
I looked at the calendar it was Mother's Day
Lucky I got the mail on the special day.

I didn't have patience for the knife to open it
Instead I tore the envelope with my bare hands.
A magnet with a picture fell from the envelope
I was perplexed by not comprehending the picture.
The poem on the card had customary motherly praise
With a loving personal note from both of them
Love you dearly Ma and the future grandma.

It was then I realized the picture was the sonogram
How they didn't reveal the fact a month earlier!
We had visited when they came to us to see the cherry blossom.
As a mother I couldn't figure out the pregnancy
Daughter-in-law was clever to conceal it so so well.
The kick of the surprise I got from the news
Raised my dopamine level without bound
Nothing ever brought so much joy.

Secret World

Eight of us—inseparable soul mates
Thirteen and fourteen with neatly braided hair
Wearing a touch of makeup and lipstick
Forbidden by our mothers.
We were known in school as unbreakable eight
Since fourth grade.
We used to wear school uniforms—green frocks
With white collars and white borders on the half sleeves.
All of a sudden we all got four inches taller
Which forced us to wear
White shalwar, green kameez with white collars
And white borders on full sleeves.
We covered our newly acquired raised chests
With white folded dopatta.

Nargis brought a book she stole from her mother's drawer
Engraved in the book, *essentials for a newly wedded couple.*
Flabbergasted by the pencil sketches of nude bodies—
Whispering "I love you," kissing, and touching
We started laughing like the roars of Niagara Falls.
Taken aback by our craziness the other students
Rushed to us with annoyance and curious looks.
The book vanished in a blink,
It was the first time we were exposed
To a secret world.

Delights

The craft of getting delights in the day to day isn't hard;
So many good things happen every day
It would be hard to keep track of them.

Try to find delight every day. Pay attention to
A bird's nest filled with eggs on the ledge,
Or a poised deer standing middle of the road at dawn,
Or a mother licking all its kittens under the deck,
Without doubt brought delight.

Pay more attention to the all-around activities:
A gym instructor gives a high five for weight lifting,
Or a student gives a thank-you card,
Or a little girl holds tightly the hand of an old man,
All of them certainly brought pleasure.

Even on a subzero day, waiting for a bus, cold breeze
Made my hands and feet numb through so many layers
But when I entered the heated bus
No words could describe the delight.

Vivacious

47

Hear ye! Hear ye! The morning sun
Announced its warmth in the Siberian city.
The icicles hanging from the rooftop
Gleaming into the windowpane
Hauling the insanity out of the mind.
The heart started roiling in gratitude
To the omnipotent for a flaunted gaudy day,
Last night's dream transpired after the blizzard.

Question

Nine servings of fruits and vegetables daily
Supposedly keep a doctor away.
What is a serving, I wonder?

Strawberries, blueberries, black blackberries
Work wonders to keep the memory sharp.
Bananas and potatoes loaded with potassium
Reduce blood pressure without any question.
Avocadoes loaded with vitamins, minerals, healthy fat
The advice is to have it regularly in a meal.
Citrus fruits rich in vitamin C and flavonoids
Fight the common cold and improve gut health.
Green leafy vegetables, green leafy vegetables
Make the bones strong and keep cancer away.
Carrots are a great source of vitamin A
Good for eyes nutritionists suggest.
Broccoli and cauliflower are high in fiber
Have them control blood sugar.
Tomatoes, sweet potatoes with their eye-catching hues
Make the skin soft without any blemish.

Nine servings of fruits and vegetables
Nine Servings of fruits and vegetables
I do not have room to eat anything else!

A Picture

On her fortieth birthday, I decided
To give my daughter, Lily, a photographic album.
Sorting through piles of pictures
I wanted to choose those reflecting
Special moments in her growing up.
A picture of when she was three
Reminded me of my parents' house in Dhaka.

It was the first colored photograph of Lily
Taken by Ripon, my brother, from the US.
All our prior photographs were black and white
The colored film cost a fortune then.
Ripon came *home* after five years,
Lily and I came to my parents' house
To spend a few days with him.

Ripon left home to do internship at a Michigan hospital
Got a job at the end of the program.
He was afraid to visit *home* prior to receiving
His permanent residency visa to the US.
A few of his acquaintances were denied
Reentry without the visa.
He wanted to settle in the US,
Didn't want to jeopardize it by *emotional expenses.*

Lily was on the bed
Covered by a blue and white striped bed sheet.
A portion of a couch seen in the picture
The red cushion covers were made by my mother.

She decorated the headrests (not seen in the picture) with pink Aida
fabric
Embroidered them with cross and herringbone stitches
And used green, blue, and red threads.

Lily was three wearing a red cloak (a gift from her uncle)
Ripon put a couple of Barbie books on her chest
Before taking the picture.
But somehow he didn't pay attention to
The mosquito net still hanging on the side of the bed.
No one paid any attention to the clutters,
Everyone was eager to know Ripon's
Experiences in a dreamland.

The angel-faced little girl now, soon will turn forty
A recent photograph showed her
With confident smile wearing a lab coat.

Mango

A soft ripe one, rub it with two hands until
the flesh turns into a pulp. You can feel
the smoothness of the pulp under the skin.
Then, make a whole at one end. Squeeze it
and suck the pulp like a child sucking.
It tastes like amrita or ambrosia—
described in the Hindu or Greek mythology.

A green one, cut into small pieces, and
boil with water and sugar until tender.
Cool the liquid. The drink on a hot summer day
quenches the thirst and cools the body.
Ma used to make pickles with the green ones.
In a jar she soaked the small pieces and spices
in mustard oil and kept the jar in sunlight
for couple of weeks.

Mango, I love thee, whole-heartedly.
When I first moved to the US
you were not available in any stores.
I craved for you like a newly wedded bride—
waiting for a call from her beloved.

Painting

Beauty by Zainul Abedin

Her head is resting on her knees, her eyes are closed.
I wonder if she is sitting in the backyard after a day's work.

The painting reminded me of a housewife in Bengal
Who after the day's work took a shower and
Put on a red woven saree her husband bought.
She wore the red matching bangles and
Colored her feet and toenails by *alta.*
Her husband bought cosmetics, jewelry
From the village market
After selling potatoes, cauliflowers, beans,
Chickens and eggs produced on his farm.
He toiled hard in the farm so to buy
Presents for his love of life.

Looking at the mirror the woman in the painting
Cherished her beauty
With satisfaction she began dreaming.

About the Author

Dipa Sarkar-Dey was born and raised in Dhaka, Bangladesh. After completing her MSc in pure mathematics from the University of Dhaka, she became a lecturer of mathematics in the Accounting department of her alma mater. She came to the USA as a graduate student and completed her MSE and PhD in mathematical sciences from the Johns Hopkins University. Currently, she is an associate professor emerita of the Mathematics and Statistics Department at Loyola University Maryland. She was awarded the Fulbright teaching/research scholarship twice.

She has been writing and publishing nonfiction as well as fiction for a while. However, she began writing poetry after retirement.

www.ingramcontent.com/pod-product-compliance
Lightning Source LLC
Chambersburg PA
CBHW031001180726
47993CB00018B/1359